Daylily Coloring Book

Heidi Thorne

ISBN-13: 9798718032628

Thorne Communications LLC, HeidiThorne.com

Why Daylilies?

I'm a lazy "black thumb" gardener. I've tried many times over the years to get better at it. But it just isn't my thing. I'd rather be writing or reading than digging in the dirt. However, I do want a pretty garden that has some color and form.

A master gardener friend of mine suggested I try planting daylilies (hemerocallis). Some were already growing on our property, planted by previous owners. They're probably in the range of 30 years old or older. I then planted more, including some specialty varieties. Though I don't remember exactly what year I planted them, it has likely been at least 15 years. These perennial friends now grace our yard each summer with pops of yellows, oranges, reds, and pinks against fountains of spiky green foliage.

To celebrate these lovely plants, I've created the *Daylily Coloring Book*, featuring plantings from my own yard. I've regularly taken photos of them when they are in bloom. These photos were then converted into line drawings with the Colorscape mobile app. (Used with permission for this book. App is available in the Apple App Store for iOS and Google Play Store for Android, or visit their website at colorscape.co).

Daylily fans, gardeners, and coloring book enthusiasts will all enjoy coloring these pages that showcase different varieties and scenes. The pictures are highly stylized, with sufficient detail to provide you with a relaxing and engaging pastime. There are 2 sets of 36 different coloring pages so you can try out multiple color combinations.

Use whatever coloring tools you wish. However, note that very liquid markers and pens, or watercolors, may bleed through the page, damaging other pages in the book. If you do use more liquid mediums, consider using a protective layer of cardboard or other barrier material underneath your coloring page to protect the other pages.

Though you might want to stick to nature's colors when coloring, you don't have to. There are two of each coloring page so you can try different color combinations. You might even want to display some of them when you're done.

Enjoy!

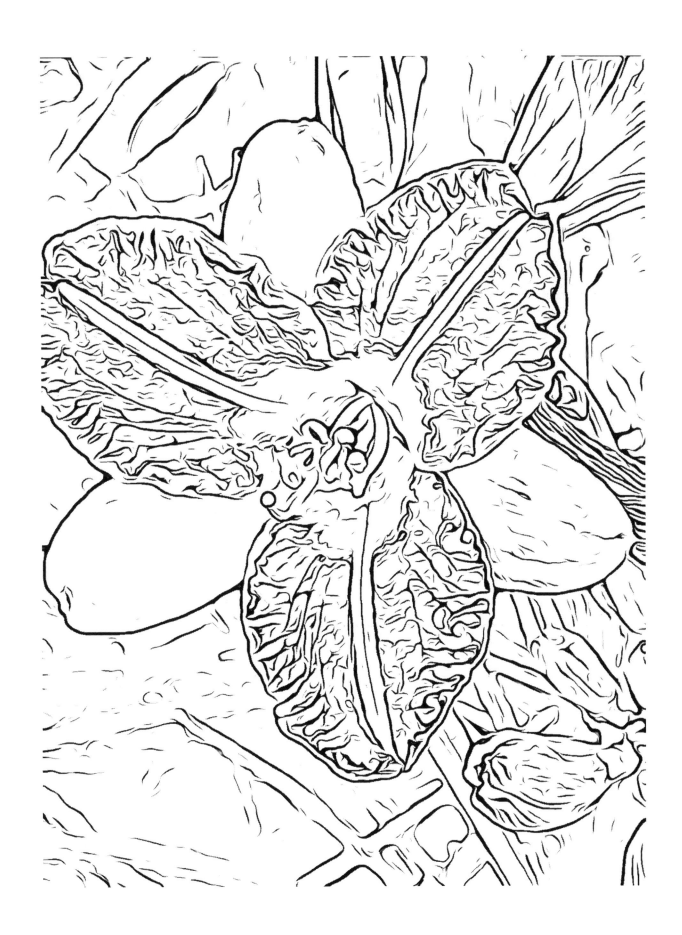

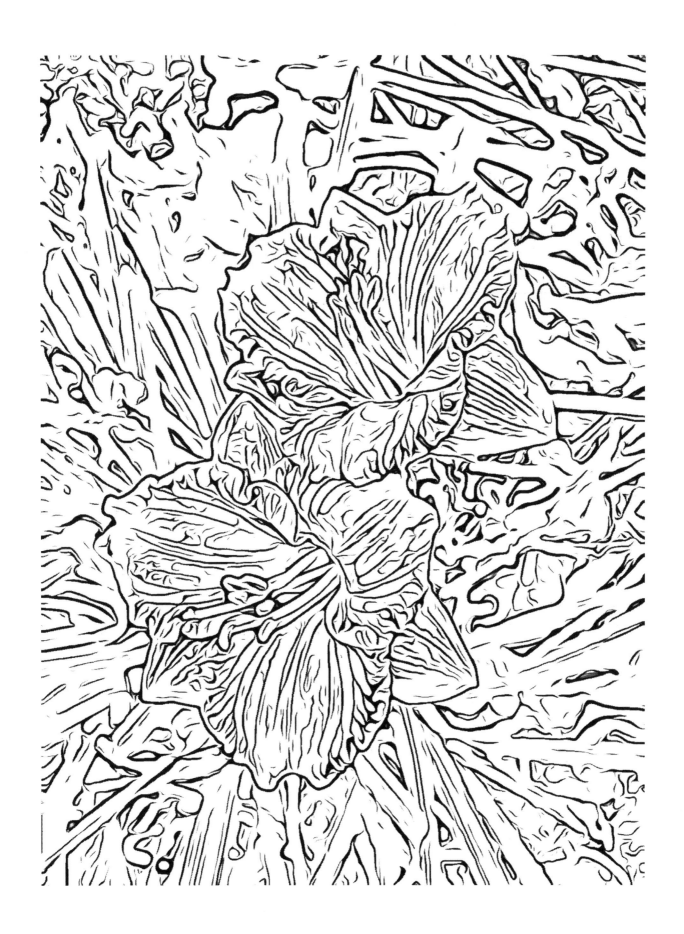

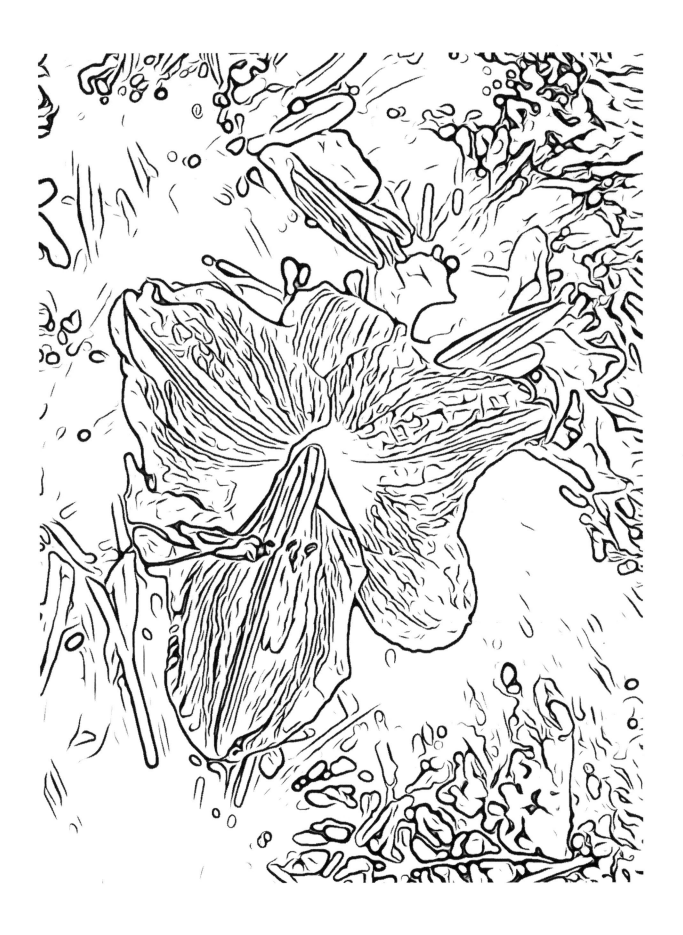

About Heidi Thorne

Heidi Thorne is a business author, podcast host, blogger, and self publishing expert. If you want to know more about what Heidi does best (which isn't gardening), visit her website at HeidiThorne.com.

Made in the USA
Columbia, SC
08 July 2025

60501115R00083